NOVELTY SALT AND PEPPER SHAKERS

FRANCES HARRIS

ACKNOWLEDGEMENTS

I would like to take this opportunity to thank my family and friends for their support during the production of this book, especially Nigel, who lent his sets and his home, and gave his patience, expertise and vast amounts of tea. (You need some more tea bags Nigel!)

Thank you everyone.

Frances.

ISBN 0-9517686-0-3

CONTENTS

INTRODUCTION

"WOULD YOU LIKE TO COME AND SEE MY CRUETS?"
Even with an agonisingly painful back, the 'pull' to see Nigel's cruets, up, what felt like ten flights of stairs, made me fall, partly from exhaustion and partly from wonderment on to the nearest chair. When I think of how I very nearly missed the first of many visits – I shudder. The experience – the opening of a new wonderful world was at my feet. There were shakers everywhere crammed close to each other. On shelves, in cupboards, on the cooker! I oohed and aahed, I'm still oohing and aahing.

This fascinating subject knows no end, no limit. There is always something different to see and to find. Nobody knows or has seen it all. That is what makes it so interesting.

Nearly everyone has a funny tale or interesting encounter which sparked off their collection.

If you ask Nigel his first impression of me, it was "I hope this woman is going to make it up these stairs!"

Well, make it I did, and I've never looked back.

As I intend this first book to be merely an introduction to this area of collecting, the subjects and sub-sections have only been touched upon. Any information to the best of my knowledge is correct, however, I am always open to correction or comment. With this being a fairly new subject in the collectors' world, let us share our information that we may all learn.

On behalf of my friends in the British Novelty Salt & Pepper Collectors' Club, welcome to this wonderful miniature world.

Advertising

In any area of collecting you will find the advertising section high on the list for value.

The obvious items, i.e. those marked with product or maker's name, are not too easy to find, and when once found remain hidden away in collections.

Less obvious items can be overlooked at first by not realising the advertising quality.

The Ken-L-Ration yellow dog and black cat set made in plastic by F. & F. Mold & Dye Work Co. of Ohio in the 1950s is a good example. Probably recognised quickly in the USA but fairly unknown in Britain.

Also made by the same company, were Aunt Jemima and Uncle Mose, given away in exchange for box tops from Quaker pancake mix. In the same series you will find spice jars, cookie jar, and syrup pitcher. The salt and pepper shakers were produced in two sizes, 3½″ and 5½″.

Beer bottles were made to promote breweries and maybe given away by the individual public houses. Look for the ones with metal tops, and the name MUTH in the base as they are worth more.

Petrol companies did the same with petrol pumps and may have had the garage name on a label.

Bullets made to promote ammunition companies had actual shell bases, with red bakelite casings. The holes in the shape of S and P were in the top. From a distance I was once asked "Are they lipsticks?" You can get a pleasant one-piece modern salt and pepper from the Happy Eater chain, not too dear and may be of interest in years to come. I've kept mine in the original box for this reason. This area is fascinating for those interested in products long forgotten, but of course, the older and more unusual sets will command a high price. Expect to pay £10+ in this section.

People

Let's face it! How far can we go without bumping into people? Life's full of them – so are salt and peppers.

This section can be divided into initial categories, i.e. Nationalities, Jobs, Hobbies etc. with many sub-divisions.

As this is only an introduction to salt and pepper shaker collecting, I will not go on at length listing some of the multitude of sets. Go out and find them for yourselves. That is the fun. I will, however, touch on the main groups to give you some idea of what to look for.

Advertising

Flower graders are not the plastic variety. People, ''Before and After'', are advertising a medicine. Stamped ''Nicholas Laboratories Ltd., 1982''. Petrol pumps – sorry, I could not find a Shell set.

People

Goebel monks. Frances and Bill Clements own the Cardinal condiment set, and Marion Sutton the pair which have ''Cardinal Tuck'' on gold labels on reverse. Also pictured, one of the brown varieties.

Nationalities

Although a lot of sets you find will be Japanese, the countries represented will be many. Of course one would expect to find beautiful oriental figures, but just as equally, attractive pairs of Dutch, Mexican, Swiss, and very popular Red Indian make a colourful display on your shelves. The greater number will have a man and a woman as the two shakers, but I have seen some lovely two-girl combinations, and in the next section quite often two-men sets.

Jobs and Pastimes

Perhaps the most easily recognisable will be the Goebel monks. Not only as salt and pepper, these were made into mustard pots, egg cups, jugs, decanters, matchbox holders and egg timers. I'm referring to the brown ones. If you find a cardinal, the red variety, you would be well advised to hang on to it. They were only made in 1951 and, therefore, limited.

In the realm of fishermen, boxers, wrestlers etc. you will find only male shakers. Some may be identical pairs, others completely different. Here, observation and experience can help. I've often drooled over a set, only to find later it wasn't such.

I have to admit I am not always sure what sex some sets are. A set of babies in nappies, with not a blue or pink bow in sight – I can only leave to your imagination!

Take care when buying to examine 'bits sticking out'. A shovel, angel's wing etc. can have been cleverly repaired. The same applies to hands, feet, and yes, even heads.

Some people would class sunbathing as a leisure pastime, which leads nicely into the 'naughty bits' or *risqué* sets.

People

Three back row sets are German, front two Japanese. Centre set are "Happy and Sad".

People

Gandhi's partner is just his head, but we used artistic licence as the remainder were complete figures.

Naughty, Naughty

It depends upon just how broad your mind is, but I like to think this section is rude but not smutty.

Certain items appear presentable when viewed solely from the front, but turn them around, or have a mirror behind them, and you will notice that all is not as it seems. I do not own any of these (at the moment).

It would not be correct for me to describe these items in detail – anyway I wouldn't dream of spoiling your fun when you do find them.

And if you do – let me have a look!

Turnabouts

I have put these into the 'People' section, as I have yet to find any that fall into any other category. The theme is *Before and After*, i.e. a young couple on their wedding day, turned, become a middle-aged or elderly couple.

This is another section which I find is enhanced when displayed in front of mirror tiles, so that you can view both sides all the time.

Do enjoy your people. If you like Dutch figures, you could make a whole collection consisting solely of these. There are so many different sets, many under £10, and the expressions on some of the faces defy you to be miserable.

If it is quality not quantity you want, why not collect the Goebel children figures. These vary between £20–£30 per pair or set, but do examine them carefully for even the slightest damage. All dealers do not point out defects, whereas some are very good on this point.

A collection made up of musicians is a marvellous talking point. There is usually an instrument somebody has attempted to play at some time.

People – Indians

Two Indians with tepees are slightly different. Indian set on L has mustard as centre figure. Centre set at back – building is mustard.

Naughty, Naughty

Where did these come from? They are not mine. The man's hand is part of the girl shaker, and the lady's bosom is part of the man shaker.

People

The central set in back row is Sandra Webb's, and sits nicely with the others of this kind.

People

Joyce Culling owns the three wooden sets, the mounties (Japanese) are Greta Haywood's, the little couple (actually a condiment set) is Frances Clements', and the girl with flowers belongs to Marion Sutton. A real club members' picture.

Babies

Pairs extreme R and L are Japanese copies of the Rose O'Neill Kewpie dolls (German) which the rest are, with the exception of front set which are early German.

People

All these are from the collection of Christine Edwards. Mr. Macawber and Sairey Gamp are Beswick, the remainder Goebel. Christine kindly had these photographed herself, due to the distance involved.

Animals

I would divide the animal kingdom into two very definite sections:

1. Realistic. Those that look exactly like the animal they are supposed to be.
2. Comic or dressed animals.

Realistic

If you are an animal lover, this is your forte. You can have a menagerie of any animals that take your fancy, or be selective and collect just one species. Be warned, if you are a cat fanatic you will not find as many sets as you might hope, especially when I tell you that club member David Brown collects only cat cruets. So we know where a lot of them are!

Animals are included in other sections such as: squirrels hanging on a tree (hangers), or mothers with babies (nesters). I have covered these later in the book.

To enable you to be selective, you can divide this subject into domestic, woodland, wildlife, zoo, circus etc. Look in the right places and you can find animal sets from as little as £2 upwards. I am keeping the prices at the lower end of the market for now, but you can spend well over £100 for good sets later if you desire. I feel between £5 and £10 is a reasonable amount if you are buying on a regular basis, and there are lots of appealing little animals in this price range if you search. As with the 'people' sets you will often find a male/ female pair e.g. stag and deer, two similar in different poses, or two identical but with identifying holes for salt and pepper.

Some makes will be more expensive, but not necessarily more attractive. As many people have said to me, "I buy what I like to look at, regardless of who made it. After all, I've got to live with it." I wholeheartedly agree.

Animals – Cats

Part of David Brown's collection of cats. Does anyone have the partner to the little fellow with the fiddle?

Animals – Condiment Sets

Three little pigs (centre). Dogs listening to radio headphones, first of its kind (left). Three dogs on tray (right).

Comic or Dressed

A subject wide open to the Mr. and Mrs. theme. He with cap and trousers, she with bonnet, long dress and pinafore. Some people love these as they find them so appealing, other cannot stand them. It's personal isn't it? So is your collection. If you like them – buy them.

Most of you must have seen the modern sets of bears in little bibs etc. Bear collectors buy salt and pepper shakers just to add to their bear collection. You should not pay more than £4–£5 for sets like these.

I have a very attractive Goebel grey rabbit in my own collection. He is holding a carrot which is nearly as big as he is. Value at present approximately £15–£18.

Animals made of red clay are painted in high gloss black with red trimming. There are long lanky cats and little sheep with cap and bonnet to name a couple, but the detail is not easily recognisable.

Some animals have coloured glass or rhinestones for eyes and trimming. Do not think the male has lost an eye. If you look closely you will find he is sporting a monacle.

Although two items can make up one set, sometimes two items only make up one pet. Such an example is the dachsund, split into two and measuring 7½" from nose to tail.

Interesting items are, cat carrying two kittens in a basket, dog half-in/out kennels, dogs wrapped around lamp-posts, giraffes with interlocking necks, various animals with interlocking tails. I am not too keen on animals covered in flowers, the painted-on variety, but that is just a personal feeling.

Here is probably a good place to include calico dogs and cars, and patchwork animals. Not too pricey, although there are not many about in this country.

Why not give a few pets a good home?

Animals

I know – the corgi standing with the Goebel animals is NOT a cruet. She is there to appeal to anyone who has the Goebel pair of corgis. Please, I have a collector begging for it. (That is the position of the shakers.)

Animals – Pigs

There are lots of people who love and collect pigs, so these are just for you.

Animals

Bonzo-type dogs made by Royal Worcester for American market. £400 per set. Six dogs on stools are ''Bar Hounds''.

Animals

Boxer dogs by Goebel belong to Frances Clements. Squirrel with cone is Goebel, and is one of many of this kind. Bambies are owned by Kath Brown, and the bears are mine.

Animals

Seven sets of dressed animals and birds from the same series. German. There is also a set of dressed ducks.

Animals

How can you be miserable when you study this assortment of expressions?

Birds

To my mind, this is one of the most colourful topics you could choose. You cannot be sad with these cute little faces gracing your abode. Let us not forget the farmyard birds – turkeys, chicks, roosters, and the water fowl, quaint little ducks, geese, mallard, pheasants etc. We all know how popular are the cartoon characters like Daffy Duck, and Foghorn Leghorn etc. These have not escaped the salt and pepper shaker manufacturer's whim.

Owl collectors are particularly well catered for here. They (the owls not the collectors) come in all shapes, sizes and positions. The most realistic sets are birds perched upon branches.

Swans grace any collection, and they do not escape the shaker market. Display your swans, ducks etc. on mirrors, and enjoy the reflection of these beautiful creatures.

Fish and Water

Move along your mirror into deeper water. Dive beneath the surface, and here you have a beautiful array of all kinds of fish. Some are made in heavier ceramic, but if you seek out the fine bone china specimens, they are so delicate that I think you tend to judge the others as coarse (an apt term for anglers).

Prices £4–£10 for Japanese. Nice little pair of blue fishes on a tray by Goebel would probably cost £8–£12.

Around any water you will soon find another very popular subject – FROGS. Loads of them. On lily pads, under toadstools etc., and even on each others backs. I have a very realistic pair of toads, but the one in front appears to be lost, as the one behind is pushing it!

One collector in Pennsylvania, whom I have had the great pleasure to meet, collects only anything water-related. It is amazing when you think how many things have a water connection, such as alligators, hippos, ships (see 'Transport'), umbrellas, taps etc. Yes these are all salt and pepper shakers.

Birds

A truly 'club member's' selection. Joy Coleman's pheasants on tray are Carlton, Marion Sutton's chicks/hen on basket are market 'Foreign', whilst her birds on tree branch are Japanese. Sandra Webb's chicks in broken egg are hand-painted and her set centre back are Japanese.

Birds

Around the world with this lot. From flamingos and penguins, to good old farmhouse chicken with her eggs.

Birds – Owls

Especially for owl lovers. Two side sets are early 1900, by Conta and Boehme.

Birds

Duck collectors will love this condiment set. I tried to keep all the owls together but this pair have flown in from the owl picture.

Birds

Chickens and ducks are one of the most attractive things to collect. The pair on the tray are Goebel.

Birds

Are the toucans listening to the two birds in song? Look at the expression on the ducks!

Water-related

Condiment set is Goebel and is also available as a pair. Ducks and trough set marked "Foreign". Nessie is KPG (England) and owned by Joyce Culling.

"Lavatories"

There is always one that lowers the tone! I told you no subject could escape being made into a shaker set. I suppose this has to be water-related.

Water – Frogs

The spoon in the mustard forms a flower bud. The musical frogs are all two-piece shakers including the nester (second L).

Water – Frogs

Don't let frogs hop away. Very collectable and prices are rising.

Transport

These days any form of transport is looked on as a necessity as opposed to the luxury it was considered to be in the earlier days of shaker mania.

In ceramic ware, you have a vast choice of vehicles from early stage coaches, covered wagons, cars, ships, trains, buses, and aeroplanes. To bring it right up to date the space age is not forgotten, with rockets, UFOs, and if you consider they fit into this slot, the earth, moon and stars.

Quite a common, but nevertheless interesting item, is an ocean liner which comes in many sizes and details, and often has "A present from . . ." in gold on one side. The funnels and steam form the centre handle, with the pepper and mustard at each end and the salt in the middle. Likewise two sailing ships sitting on the waves make an attractive set especially when placed near a three-piece stacking lighthouse.

A locomotive with the funnels as the salt and pepper stayed with me for approximately 24 hours before being snapped up by a railway enthusiast.

If you like the metal/plastic combination, you could be the proud owner of a model T Ford, complete with box if you are lucky. (Boxed sets are listed separately.)

For transport-related items you may see a foot pump with flat tyre (go with) and not forgetting the petrol pumps (advertising). Many subjects are inter-relating, and one set could appear in several sections and be equally at home.

The Japanese-made donkey carts laden with fruit, vegetables or flowers. The donkey is lead by boy or girl, and only the fruit etc. is removable to form the shakers, the rest being a one-piece base. There are some more modern sets marked 'Foreign', but if the set is complete and attractive, I'd buy it. Prices can range from £8–£15, but make sure the shakers match and have not just been made up to make the set appear complete.

I have not seen many aeroplane sets, and those I have bought have sold almost immediately. Ray Dodd let me have a delicate set – one black and one white 'plane on a tray. Have you got another one Ray?

Zeppelins, submarines etc. were manufactured in the seaside momento and crested items. Obviously the subject matter raises the price of these. If you find them, be prepared to pay £25–£40 per item.

Transport

Transport through the ages. Stagecoach – vintage car – aeroplane. The ship is the more commonly seen set.

Transport

All mustard transport sets. The dog's mustard is in the boot, and the people's in the bonnet. More ususual version of the ship set.

Food

With salt and pepper being food-related, it is natural that you would expect to be spoilt for choice here, and you certainly will not be disappointed.

Fast food fans can collect hot dogs, hamburgers, jacket potatoes with butter, and finish off with a chocolate milk shake (plastic). You like bread? Two loaves each with a prayer on the side, or toast popping out of toaster. How about a cake with a slice cut, one being salt, the other pepper. This is a miniature set (yet another section).

I must put the fruit and vegetables in here, although many collectors treat them as a subject apart. The more you see of them the more you understand why. You name the fruit or veg. and you will find it somewhere as a shaker. A very colourful theme that will fit in with any colour scheme and brighten your kitchen. Extend this further, and you can enter the realm of fruit and vegetable people. Some have just a face incorporated into the whole fruit, i.e. apple or bunch of grapes, whereas some take the idea to the fantasy world and use the fruit as a head surmounted on a body which then partakes in an activity, such as playing a musical instrument. Personally, I can't say that I find a head shaped like a banana appeals to even my sense of humour. But there are many and various sets to give you hours of pleasure without moving from this subject.

Prices for ceramic sets £5+. Wooden sets can be found for as little as £2.

Food

Loaves (Carlton Ware), eggs and cups in foreground are all one, whereas face eggs sit in cups and are Japanese. These are owned by Joyce Culling.

Fruit and Vegetable People

Fruit and vegetable people pairs. All Japanese.

Buildings and Places

Among the most attractive in this section must be the windmills, in blue and white with movable sails. Some are Delft, so you do need to look at the mark underneath. Some sails are metal, but the pottery ones need careful handling.

Three cottages on a tray, mainly brown, include a mustard pot and vary in age. There are also matching teapots, cheese dishes etc.

The earlier Japanese brightly-coloured sets were made into some very nice combinations such as a windmill, where only the top is the pepper, and the little house alongside is the salt. Price £12.

As regards shakers in the actual shape of the landmark, you are more likely to find American subjects, e.g. Shrine of Democracy, Niagara Falls etc. Apart from the ever-popular Blackpool Tower, most places in Britain appeared as a coloured transfer on a pair of binoculars or a boat. At one time you could pick these up for £3–£4 but I have noticed recently they have crept up to £10–£12.

If you prefer the natural rugged look, a tin mine made of two pieces would appeal to you. Painted in a greenish-brown, it comprises the building and chimney, and I believe it was made in Cornwall.

So there are many different things for you travellers to watch out for.

Buildings

One of the attractions of Greta's Tower of London is that it is unbreakable. Note the little canons at each side of the tower set.

Buildings

Lighthouse and boat are shakers, and house mustard.

Black Americana

This highly-collectable subject in America does not seem widely known in Britain. In the 1950s it was taboo to stereotype certain races and the production of shakers and other items in that vein was stopped.

Some of the pieces are extremely charming and I am pleased to own a little boy holding his oversized piece of water-melon. He is the salt and the melon the pepper. Value approximately £15.

Slightly more available are the two children playing in a basket, and prices can range from £8–£12.

The Aunt Jemima and Uncle Mose already detailed in the advertising section fit into the category of Black Americana.

Black Americana

Four completely different styles if you want to specialise in this area. R-hand set, mouth is open salt.

Black Americana

Heads on tray are nice quality, but often are incomplete or damaged.

Christmas

To some people every day is Christmas. Why? Because they collect solely Christmas items. Well, in our field there is a truly wonderful array of Christmas shakers in which I include snow people.

Santa and Mrs. Claus in varying poses would make a collection alone, but add Christmas trees, presents, angels, bells, puddings, and why not churches, to make a whole seasonal area in your collection. Add tinsel or holly, and you do not need to spend a fortune on other decorations when the season actually comes round.

You do need to search a little for these sets, so be prepared to pay a little more when you are successful.

Christmas

Not the 12 days of Christmas, but 12 delightful angels in different poses. The holes are centred in the haloes.

Christmas

The two outer Santas should hang on either side of a tripod and go with the cauldron. The Santa with sack makes a lovely Christmas 'go with'.

Oriental

To collectors of anything oriental, may I say please add salt and pepper shakers to your pieces.

You may already have the usually accepted standard items, i.e. three identical patterned items on matching tray, the small Noritake sets or a pair of quite serviceable shakers.

But please look at some of the novelty shakers, and you will see pieces to enhance your other items.

Some couples such as the seated pair in green coats, red hats, and reading books, look very good quality but are only about £10–£12. Alternatively, a wooden set where the head is attached by a spring gives a very eastern look when in motion and costs around £7–£8.

Some are just heads, i.e. Geisha and Boy, and on this size the face is important to make the set attractive. On the full figures often the face is only suggested by the merest lines.

Occupied Japan

Again another specialist subject. There is even an Occupied Japan Collectors' Club in America.

All items are dated from 1945 (end WWII) to 28th April, 1952, and are marked 'Made in Occupied Japan' on the base. I recently acquired the canoe (marked) containing the Indian and squaw which were only marked 'Japan'. However, I understand this is only because there would not have been room to print in full on the shakers.

As long as the shakers are the correct ones for the base, and the base is marked 'Made in Occupied Japan', your set is bona fide. There are all sorts of things to look for if you want to collect a particularly dated period like this.

Prices range from £10–£40 depending upon availability.

Oriental

Small selection of oriental figures. There are many more, and all rather attractive.

Occupied Japan

Watermill is housed with Sandra Webb. These are just a few of the O.J. items you can find.

Mustard Sets

Nigel, our Chairman of the British Novelty Salt and Pepper Collectors' Club, who has amassed a staggering 14,000 sets, has decided to concentrate on mustard, or condiment sets for his next 14,000. It is a wonderful feeling to find a set he hasn't got, and then tell him he can't have it! (for 5 minutes at least).

Having seen some of his amazing sets, I would say to the beginner, start with something else. Unless you want to start paying out £35–£50 for a decent set.

Of course you can find cheap little mustard sets, like a group or orange mushrooms, on a green base at approxmately £5–£6, or a house (mustard) with out-house (pepper) and water wheel (salt) at approximately £15–£16, but put them at the side of a really good set and you will not be content with the cheapies.

In many cases the china spoons have long gone and it is amusing what appears in their place. But if you buy a set, please keep whatever spoon is in it, at least until you get home. I have found that many heads, i.e. mustard lids, will not sit properly without a spoon, and you do not want to provoke damage.

People – Condiment Sets

Fine selection of clowns. The one carrying weights has removable head. Also note priest with bride and groom, and chef with waiter and waitress.

Condiment Sets

The two girl figures extend into the suitcase, but they are also available with flat bottoms as a pair. Dog cart has nodding head by Conta and Boehme.

Condiment Sets

Yet another Indian set. Girl with eggs does not always have the chicken alongside. Pigs are joined. Back row – Japanese. Front row – German.

People – Condiment Sets

In each set the top half of the large figure is removed for mustard pot, and heads of small figures are the shakers.

Condiment Sets

Back row. L Peter Piper. Centre Humpty Dumpty. R Pussy Cat. Pussy Cat where have you been? Front L Arabs and Camels. Front R Mother Goose.

Miscellaneous Condiment Sets

Sandra Webb's beehives are Royal Winton (Grimwades, England) and Joyce Culling lent the men's heads on the tray. Lady is mustard, flower pots, the shakers. Sedan is mustard, flunkeys the shakers made in Czechoslovakia. Golfers are German.

Novelty – Novelty

Please bear with me while I drool in what is my favourite area. As there are quite a few similarities between the groups, it is important to know the differences which divide the sections, therefore, each making a collecting topic in which you can specialise.

Nodders

These all have a base used just for housing the nodders. I demonstrate these by standing with my hands on my hips and say, "Imagine my head is the only part of the shaker you see, my extended shoulders the notches on which the container rests, and the rest of my body swings inside the base making the visible part nod."

A very common base was white, decorated with flowers (often pink) with PATENT TT raised on the base. A variety of fish, animals, and birds nodded on the top. To give you an idea of size, a fawn salt or pepper would be as big as the last joint of my little finger.

Among my kangaroos I am lucky enough to have the nodder. The mother's head is the pepper and rocks forward and back, whilst the baby is the salt and rocks side to side.

As you move on to the more unusual items, the price can rise into the £100+ bracket. Probably not something for the absolute beginner, but definitely sets to have in the back of your mind for the future. If you ever see a cheap nodder, get it, there will always be some one who wants it. That is if you are prepared to part with it. We get very possessive about our 'finds'.

Wonderful subject – highly collectable.

Nodders

Frances and Bill have a lovely collection, and have included three nodders – Irish children, fish, and hen/cock on decorated base. Teamed with Nigel's monkeys, cowboy and children, they make a super picture.

Nodders

The two Souvenir of Mexico sets have mustard pots in the centre. Elephant set is superb. Irish couple are complete figures.

Nesters

A nester has one piece resting on top of the other, or two pieces resting in a base but not just sitting on a tray, e.g. two birds sitting on or in the branch of a tree. It is important that, in the two-piece sets, the top item does not touch the ground surface.

My collection is made up mostly of nesters, so I am being extremely careful not to go on at length and bore you, as I feel I could fill the whole book on this section alone.

Having wanted the hyacinth in its flower pot for some time, I saw it at Nigel's, found it was Goebel, and it took me 2 days to prise it out of his hand.

My long-suffering sister Kath, who painstakingly wraps and unwraps all my sets at the collectors' fairs, found another of my 'wanted' sets – Niagara Falls. The base comprises part of the falls with the *Maid of the Mist* in the foreground, and the whole falls splits into two to form the shakers which rest on the base, all beautifully painted. Thank you Kath for a wonderful birthday present.

Just a few more sets to illustrate nesters – chicken sitting in roasting pan, typewriter on desk, rabbit in cabbage, a half-peeled banana. I pay anything around £10 per set but am always happy to find cheaper ones.

Nesters

Five different animals driving their motors. Car – salt. Animal – pepper. I have a rabbit set with upright ears in this mode.

Nesters

I have split Frances Clements' turkey and nest to show you the eggs. Kangaroo is common, but some tails are straight out, and some curled. Record player – record and arm are the shakers.

Hangers

Look for a tree and you should find two things hanging from it. They could be fruits, monkeys, bears, squirrels or birds etc. They don't sit – they dangle!

Not too common. If you find a cheap set, make sure the pieces are from the same set or they will not hang correctly, and will jump off all over the place.

Carriers

Here you are, something for 50p upwards. Usually donkeys which have the salt and pepper containers hooked on the sides. I find that unless you stick these on, they do tend to fall off easily, especially when transporting to fairs, talks etc. But because they are cheaper and easier to find, don't let that put you off collecting them. What is in abundance today, can be in short supply tomorrow. The times I have said "If only I had kept that". Don't we all?

Swingers

The base is often 'U' shaped and the top 'T' shaped, so when 'T' is placed upon 'U', 'T' swings. How clever! Except, when I had a set, the holes in the base (pepper) were set so close to the ground, the pepper would have run out. Not practical, but who would want to spoil it by putting anything in it.

At around £20 per set, probably not a starter item.

Hangers and Carriers

The tree house is mustard and the hangers are the salt and pepper. All the remaining sets have removable heads for the mustard. Milkmaids, R is Bisque. L is German.

Hangers

Some of Nigel's sets. The top of elephant is mustard pot. Head is removable on front figure (bisque). L is Goebel.

Huggers

These are two items BOTH resting on the ground surface and hugging each other. They can be different, e.g. donkey hugging a bale of hay, or various animals hugging a dustbin, or two alike items which fit together. Best known are the Van Tellingen which you will often find are marked with the name round the base of the figures. There is a modern set available at the moment featuring two ducks wrapped around each other. Worth approximately £4–£6, a good starting point if you like hugging.

Squeakers

Bit of a disappointing lot as not many squeakers squeak.

I believe these contain the same kind of mechanism that were put into dolls to make them say "MA-MA".

Mainly the sets are made of wood, with the majority of the piece housing the squeak, and a very small area for the salt and pepper. The tops unscrew to fill, and if you cannot stand wood 'squealing' don't bother. You will get more noise from the thread of the wood than from the squeaker. Subjects include Africans, cats etc. Prices £3+.

Movable

I mention this to let you know there is such a thing, but I have yet to study it further.

To give you an example of this category: a lawnmower (plastic) which when pushed activates two pistons, salt and pepper, which move up and down; mechanical figures, which, when wound will walk along. An item from the boxed sets could fit in here – a piano, which, when the keys are pressed, pops the salt and pepper shakers out of the lid.

Cost can be £10–£15 for such sets.

Huggers and Squeakers

The cats are squeakers and the other two huggers. These were all that were available for the photo session.

Hangers and Miscellaneous

Joyce Culling owns this rather different set of binoculars. Nice change from the lustre sets. Lanterns are Japanese and belong to Greta Haywood.

Boxed Sets

Ironically, I have seen many boxed sets, minus box, which is why it is good to hang on to any box you get now for future reference.

Light bulbs came in both clear and opaque glass in varying colours. In the plastic field, hat-stands, hats being salt and pepper, televisions, turn the knobs and the shakers appear out of the top, and many more from the 1950s era.

I have seen these prices vary between £10–£25, depending on subject, availability, condition, and cost to vendor.

Go Withs

A little study can make this a very interesting topic and very popular with many collectors.

Two pieces totally different that 'go with' each other. As you can imagine, you can find one piece and have absolutely no idea what its partner could be. Some are obvious, i.e. lock and key, but all sets are not so easily located.

In America they have each of the states with a corresponding item, and there are two series already. Wouldn't it be nice to have all the counties of the British Isles, both the old and the new?

Even if you do not want to specialise, a few 'go withs' will add interest to your collection now, and make a good start if you want to increase the quantity later.

Prices: £5–£7 for cheaper sets.

Boxed Sets

A little different from the normal boxed plastic sets. We have raised the toby set for you to see them better.

Go Withs

The lobster set is Joy Coleman's, and the poodle/kennel one of my own favourites. Pity the poor chap in the doghouse!

One Piece

Another of our founder members of the club, Frances Clements and her husband Bill, share an interest with me in this section. The shaker has two chambers, each with its own stopper, and when shaken one way will dispense the salt, and shaken in the other direction, the pepper. Sometimes you will see S or P printed near the holes. Frances and I both have a set which is two leeks, the salt has two holes in the leaf end, the pepper three holes in the root end of the other leek. Cork stoppers and Japan in black on one leek. My pepper holes have not been punched right through. Value approximately £6.

A concertina in black, gold and blue is another interesting item. Nigel has the bell boy in all three colours. The suitcases being the two compartments. Lovely quality.

One Piece

Frances Clements lent the two central figures which are unusual. Note the birds feeding their young, both Goebel. Another version of the three wise monkeys.

One Piece

Nice variety of one-piece items. Cat/fish is interesting. Concertina and couple facing are from my collection. Back L and front R sets are German.

Miniatures

Ideal if you do not have much room. Many items are 1½″ or less and are mostly 'go withs', e.g. ring/licence, album/camera, lamp/bible, thimble/thread. These are expected to be too small to use but fascinating to look at. If you are visiting America you may be able to pick these up cheaper, but in Britain you may have to pay upwards of £15 per set.

Miniatures

A small selection of the numerous topics. Made by Arcadia Ceramics.

Miniatures

Miniatures by Arcadia Ceramics, originally supplied in dome.

Things

I always like a 'Thing' section.

Although many of the following items would easily fit into other sections, here are a few to widen your scope and show you what you could be overlooking because you didn't realise it was a shaker.

Set of books in stand. Pair book ends. Soda syphons. Boiled egg. Plugs in socket. Tenpin and ball. Musical instruments. Coal bucket and stove. Binoculars. Feet. Boots. Hats. Telephone. Nursery items. etc. etc. etc.

Substances

If you prefer to collect shakers made of one particular thing, here are some ideas:

Celluloid, Bakelite, Plastic, Wood, Metal (incl. Stainless Steel, Pewter, Silver), Glass, Chalk, Clay, Red Clay, Bone China, Ceramic, Leather, Magnets, Marble.

Combinations: Glass/China, Glass/Metal, Glass/Plastic, Plastic/Metal etc.

Trimming: Ribbon, Beads, Fur, Lace, Wool etc.

The remaining pictures contain some very attractive sets which could fit into their own subject headings.

But most people enjoy browsing through an assortment, so be my guest and wander among the pages at your leisure.

Nursery

Humpty Dumpty (marked 'Collectable Porcelain') from Joyce Culling's collection. Top L German. Top R Made in Germany for export to France. Front row German.

Disney

Only six of the seven dwarfs, but can you name them? Condiment set is Wadeheath.

Flower – Fruit People

Three fruit head people sets. Three flower head people sets. Usual Goebel quality.

Flowers and Fruit

Marion Sutton owns the old strawberry set, and although it shows some damage, still has its original spoon. The two small baskets are Marotumo ware of Japan. Front two have open salts. German.

Miscellaneous

Rabbits by Wade. Clowns by H. Wain, Longton, Stoke-on-Trent. Sailors belong to Greta Haywood. Figures on tray have flat fronts.

Gaming

Dice, chess, and the suits, along with Joyce's playing cards make a good gaming picture. Only one thing seems to be missing. THE MONEY.

Telephone

These are all mustard sets but I have a nester telephone where the base is pepper and receiver salt.

Pixies

Pixies, elves and gnomes are usually very quickly snapped up, especially in complete sets like these.

Plastic/Metal

Janet de Wagt let us picture her birds, urns and little plastic set bottom R. T.V. set would pop the shakers out of the top when the knob is turned.

Miscellaneous

Boy and girl shakers sit on mustard chair. Seat lifts off to reveal mustard pot.

Miscellaneous

The two people go with the building (front), which is the mustard. R and L buildings are by Sitzendorf. The heads sticking out of the windows are the spoon handles. Very special items.

Convention Sets – USA

Hand holding globe. 2nd Collectors' Convention Commem. set. Pittsburg, Pennsylvania, 1987. Raisin Bran with nodding raisins/3rd Convention set, Battle Creek, Michigan, 1988. Limited edition. 175 sets world-wide. Van with trailer on base. 4th Convention set, Cleveland, Ohio, 1989. Children on raft. 5th Convention set. Memphis, Tennessee, 1990. Designed by Rick Wisecarver of Ohio.

These sets owned by Ray Dodd.

THE SALT AND PEPPER CLUBS

---

by RAY DODD
ORGANISING SECRETARY
BRITISH NOVELTY SALT AND PEPPER COLLECTORS' CLUB

Melva Davern, the President of the American Novelty Salt and Pepper Shakers' Club, speaks for all collectors when she writes: 'The best part of collecting is the people you meet along the way.' During my years of collecting I have met many strangers and made many friends through our shared collecting interest. All collectors enjoy sharing their hobby with others and the best way to share new finds and new information is by joining a collectors' club.

In November 1989 a few collectors who had come to know each other through chance meetings at flea markets and fairs decided to get together to form a British Collectors' Club. That first meeting took place in Leamington Spa with just nine people present. Two years on and club membership is reaching towards fifty and growing each month. The club meets four times a year and provides a forum for meeting other collectors, exchanging information and of course buying, selling and exchanging salts and peppers.

Many of our members also belong to the American Novelty Salt and Pepper Shakers' Club. The American club was formed in 1987 and at present has over 800 members. The quarterly newsletter which they publish circulates in Canada, Australia and New Zealand as well as to members in the U.K.

Collecting is more fun when it is shared with others and world-wide there are thousands of salt and pepper collectors just waiting to hear from you – so join a club today – AND HAPPY COLLECTING.

Details of all the clubs (home and abroad) can be obtained from RAY DODD by writing to:

BRITISH NOVELTY SALT AND PEPPER COLLECTORS' CLUB,
'COLESHILL', CLAYTON ROAD,
MOLD, CLWYD, CH7 1SX
(S.A.E. please).

Conclusion

Well, I trust I have encouraged those of you who were on the brink to really start collecting salt and pepper shakers.

I have tried to give you an idea of some of the countless themes you could choose. As I have already pointed out, your collection is personal to you. One lady asked me the other day "What do you think I should start with?" Having tried to run through the contents of this book in approximately 60 seconds, she saw my point and chose one of my favourite little animal sets. The first of many I hope.

My efforts at present are directed to research into early English novelty sets and hopefully this information will be available for my next book, in which I want to concentrate on makes and dates.

I can be contacted through the British Novelty Salt and Pepper Collectors' Club, and I stand regularly at collectors' fairs organised by 'Four In One Promotions' of Oadby, Leicester. My card states "FRAN – THE CRUET LADY". Please come up and talk to me.

Looking forward to meeting you, happy collecting.

All prices in this book are given as a guide only, and may vary according to condition, availability, vendor's overheads and area.

Photography by Simon Photography of Warwick, England (except where stated).